Four Faces of Hysteria

Dedicated to my inspiration, my husband

A special thank-you to Professor Al Shull for the cover art

Contents

The Architect

CHARACTERS

DAVID—thirty-five-year-old man, married to Carol

CAROL—thirty-three-year-old woman, married to David

EAR DOCTOR—fifty-year-old woman

BETTY—thirty-year-old woman, friend of Carol

PSYCHIATRIST—sixty-year-old man

JESSICA—twenty-four-year-old woman, coworker of David

LOCATION

Atlanta, Georgia

TIME

2005

Act I

<u>Scene 1</u>

Lights rise. David arrives home and puts his drawings on a table.

DAVID

(shouting)

Carol, I am home!

Carol enters the stage with a cranky look on her face.

CAROL

It is about time. You are always late. Why are you smiling? Why are you so happy?

DAVID

My design for the building in Dubai was accepted. The architectural firm is going to make me a partner. My name will be on the firm!

CAROL

Where are they going to add your name? On the toilet paper in the bathroom? I hope they are going to pay you more now.

DAVID

(frustrated)

There is no use in talking to you. I just wanted to share some good news.

David walks away from Carol.

CAROL

(screaming)

Yeah, yeah. They say you are the best architect at the firm, but as a husband...just come back and eat your dinner.

DAVID

I am not hungry anymore.

Lights off.

<u>Scene 2</u>

Lights rise. David walks into the house.

DAVID

Carol, I am home.

Nobody answers, and then he notices a note on the table.

DAVID

(speaking to himself)

She went shopping. This will give me a chance to relax.

David pours himself a glass of wine.

It was so hectic at the office today.

Carol enters the house carrying shopping bags and sees David with the wine glass in his hand.

CAROL

(Screaming)

David, I bet you are drunk! Drinking on an empty stomach. How many glasses of wine have you had?

DAVID

Relax, Carol. I had some cheese and crackers too.

CAROL

Well that is just great! You have spoiled your dinner.

DAVID

I was hungry. Please stop nagging me.
Come and sit next to me and tell me
about your day.

CAROL

I saw Betty before I went shopping.
She talked too much and did not
make any sense. She criticized her
mother-in-law and her sisters. She is
thinking of getting a job. Maybe that
will keep her busy and stop her from
complaining so much.

DAVID

OK, let's talk about something more
pleasant. Show me what you bought.

CAROL

Why bother? I don't like any of these
clothes. I don't even know why I
bought them. I am going to return
everything tomorrow.

DAVID

Put some of the clothes on. I will give you my opinion.

CAROL

Who needs your opinion?

DAVID

Forget it. I am going to bed.

CAROL

And your dinner?

David walks away.

Lights off.

<u>Scene 3</u>

Lights rise. Carol is in the living room of the house.

CAROL

(speaking to herself)

I will tell David how I feel about things as soon as he gets home tonight.

David enters the stage.

DAVID

Hello, Carol!

CAROL

We need to talk. Sit with me.

DAVID

Sure, honey.

CAROL

I feel like you don't pay attention to me most of the time.

DAVID

I try. I ask you questions, and all you do is snap at me. Now let me tell you how I feel. I am beginning to feel very angry and frustrated. I get an uneasy feeling every night when I am about to come home from work. I come home because I love you and I want to spend my evenings with you, but something has to change. Tell me what you think happened to us.

CAROL

(speaking aggressively)

It is not what happened to us. It is what has happened to you. Are you too stupid to understand that?

DAVID

Just before we got engaged, your mother told me you were difficult to live with.

CAROL

(screaming)

She told you what?

DAVID

You heard me, but I told her it did not matter because I loved you.

CAROL

(walking around the stage and screaming)

My mother betrayed me! I knew she only loved my brothers. If she were still alive, I would be at her doorstep demanding to know why she said those things. She used to tell me that

I should try to control myself. Control
myself? What in the hell do I need to
control?

DAVID

Carol, please try to relax. Come and
sit with me. Let me serve you a glass
of wine.

CAROL

David, you really upset me. Why
didn't you tell me before what my
mother said?

DAVID

Why don't you focus instead on my
response to her? I told her I wanted
to marry you because I love you.

CAROL

My mother…

Lights off.

<u>Scene 4</u>

*Lights rise. David is in his office talking on the
phone.*

DAVID

Carol, how about I pick up your
favorite bottle of wine and some
dinner on my way home from work?

Carol's voice on the speaker phone.

VOICE OF CAROL

I am not in the mood for wine, and I
don't have an appetite. You can pick
up something for yourself.

DAVID

OK.

Lights off.

Scene 5

*Lights rise. David arrives home and walks inside.
Carol immediately confronts him.*

CAROL

I know why you are coming home
early. Your boss's secretary probably
left work early to go to happy hour
with her bimbo girlfriends. You
probably joined them.

David looks down and walks away, dejected. Carol follows him.

> CAROL

You know the secretary I am referring to. She is the one with the ridiculous breast augmentation.

> DAVID

I told you before. My boss's secretary is ready to retire. She is a grandmother! Just leave me alone. I want to eat my dinner in peace.

> CAROL

Did you bring me any dinner?

> DAVID

You said you were not hungry.

David sits down and starts to eat his dinner.

> CAROL

You are selfish.

Carol walks away.

The next day.

David walks into the house.

DAVID

Hello, Carol. Look what I have for you!

CAROL

Red roses? You know I hate that color. I like yellow roses. Yellow, yellow, yellow!

DAVID

Red roses mean love and passion.

CAROL

Give them to me.

Carol grinds them up in the garbage disposal.

There goes the love and passion.

Carol walks away laughing.

DAVID

Carol, please come back and sit next to me. Let's talk.

CAROL

Serve me some wine first.

DAVID

Sure. As I was saying...

David leans over and gives Carol a passionate kiss.

CAROL

Well, that was not so bad. It was also
one kiss the bimbo secretary is not
going to get.

DAVID

I just don't understand you.

*Carol takes another sip of wine and starts to feel
tipsy.*

CAROL

David, sorry about the roses. I should
not have done that.

DAVID

Carol, do you remember when we
first met? You smiled at me so
sweetly.

CAROL

Yes, you complimented me by saying
I had pretty teeth.

They both laugh and share a kiss.

DAVID

This evening has turned out to be wonderful. We should have dinners like this every night, but maybe with a little less wine.

He laughs and looks at Carol. She has fallen asleep.

Lights off.

<u>Scene 6</u>

Lights rise. David and Carol, both very well-dressed, arrive home from an office party.

DAVID

You humiliated me at the party. You were so sarcastic in front of everybody. How do you think that made me feel?

CAROL

Several women kept looking at you. I said those things so they would leave you alone.

DAVID

I have worked with these people for years. They are my friends, and they are good people.

CAROL

(laughing)

Well, you will not have many female friends on Monday after what I said. They are going to think the worst of you.

DAVID

No, Carol. They know me better than that. They are going to think the worst of you! *(screaming)* That's right—the worst of you.

Later that day.

DAVID

(speaking to himself)

This constant nagging and belittling of me has been going on for years. I am tired of it. At times, I just hate her. I even dream about these hostile feelings that I have toward her. It scares me. I would not want to hurt her. No, I would never hurt her. I have to control my impulses.

Weekends have become horrible. As soon as I leave the office on Friday, my thoughts become hostile. I have fantasies of shooting her right in her mouth. The sound of her voice brings rage out of me. Yes, the sound of her damn voice. I have to control myself.

David and Carol are in the living room.

DAVID

Hello, Carol. Did you have a nice day?

CAROL

I don't know why I married you. You may be a great architect, but you are a horrible husband.

Carol approaches David and starts to scratch his face with her fingernails. David doubles up his fists but then walks away.

Later that day.

DAVID

(speaking to himself)

I was brought up to respect women. What the hell am I going to do? Another weekend, and I am going to spend it being beaten down by Carol. I cannot stand it anymore! I cannot beat her up! I cannot divorce her! My religion frowns on divorce, and I am personally against violence toward women.

Later that day.

David arrives home.

CAROL

You have finally arrived home! Sit down and eat your dinner before it gets cold.

David stares at Carol. He sees her lips moving, but he cannot hear anything.

Lights off.

Act II

<u>Scene 1</u>

Lights rise. David is alone in the living room.

DAVID

(speaking to himself)

I have lost my ability to hear. I should be worried, but I feel very relaxed. This is not so bad. Now I will not get upset and feel such rage when Carol speaks. In fact, I will finally be able to have peace of mind and tranquility when I am here at home. I need to send an email to my boss explaining what is happening.

David starts typing on his computer.

VOICE OF DAVID

I have developed a sudden loss of hearing. The doctor cannot see me until Wednesday, but I will not miss work. As you know, an architect need his eyes, not his ears.

VOICE OF DAVID'S BOSS

David, please do not worry. I support you. You are the best architect at the firm. We can send each other emails if we need to communicate. Just so you know, if the doctor advises you to learn how to read lips until your problem goes away, my sister-in-law works at a clinic where you can learn how to do it. If you are interested, I can call her, and I am sure she can arrange an appointment for you.

Lights off.

<u>Scene 2</u>

Lights rise. David is in the dining room with Carol.

VOICE OF DAVID

Carol must be so angry. Her lips are moving a mile per minute. Hey, this deafness is not so bad. This is the first time I have enjoyed a dinner at home in a while. I guess I am a lucky guy. This is heaven on earth.

DAVID

Carol, dinner was delicious.

Carol just stares at David as he leaves the dining room.

Lights off.

<u>Scene 3</u>

Lights rise. David is at the ear doctor's office. The doctor and David are writing notes on a pad to communicate.

VOICE OF DOCTOR

After careful examination, I have concluded that your problem is psychological and not physical.

VOICE OF DAVID

Not physical?

VOICE OF DOCTOR

Correct. There is no damage to the structure of your inner ear. I am going to refer you to a friend who is a psychiatrist. He will probably recommend that you seek speech therapy so you can read lips until you can hear again.

Lights off.

<u>Scene 4</u>

Lights rise. David enters the house smiling.

CAROL

What is the matter with you? You seem happy all the time. I bet you are carousing around with that bimbo secretary.

DAVID

Work is going well.

CAROL

(sarcastically)

I did not ask how work is going. Can't you at least give me a little attention once in a while?

Lights off.

<u>Scene 5</u>

Lights rise at the psychiatrist's office. The psychiatrist and David are writing messages on a notepad to communicate.

>   VOICE OF PSYCHIATRIST

> David, after extensive evaluation of your hearing problem, I am convinced that this is a case of psychological deafness.

>   VOICE OF DAVID

> Psychological deafness? What is that? What would cause it?

> VOICE OF PSYCHIATRIST

> In your case, it is due to prolonged mental stress. I will explain it to you in greater detail at a later date. You will have periods when your stress level is low, and you will be able to hear. But for now, I want you to continue your speech therapy and learn to read lips proficiently.

David leaves the psychiatrist's office.

DAVID

(speaking to himself)

I don't know. I don't have to hear her voice. I have peace. I miss talking to a woman, of course, as a friend. I no longer have that. My God, what am I saying? I rarely had pleasant chats with Carol.

Lights off.

<u>Scene 6</u>

Lights rise. Jessica and David are in David's office.

JESSICA

May I speak with you, David?

DAVID

(standing up)

Of course, please sit down.

JESSICA

Don't worry if you cannot hear me; we can still communicate. I have a brother who cannot hear, so I am used to communicating with someone who is deaf.

DAVID

Well, our conversations will be pretty quiet.

Jessica and David both laugh.

JESSICA

Have you heard what happened to me?

DAVID

Yes. I am sorry to hear your fiancé broke off your engagement. Everybody here feels bad for you, including me.

JESSICA

(crying)

I am sorry, but I need to talk with someone. I feel so terrible.

DAVID

I understand. There are times that I need to talk with someone too.

JESSICA

I saw your wife at the Christmas
party. You should know that nobody
believes the things she said about
you. We all know you are a good soul.
Honestly, I don't know how you put
up with her.

DAVID

Jessica, let's go for coffee after work.
I am not making a move on you; I just
want to support you in your situation.
I can understand the despair you are
going through.

JESSICA

Thank you, David. I would like that.

DAVID

Between us, I am glad that I am deaf.

JESSICA

Don't say that!

DAVID

That it is how I feel. It is worth being
deaf so I don't have to hear Carol's
voice.

JESSICA

I understand, David, but I am still
sorry that you are deaf.

DAVID

Don't be, Jessica. I am finally a happy
man. I no longer dread going home.
Jessica, I am obviously not a
psychiatrist, but I am your friend. We
can talk openly with each other.

JESSICA

Thank you, David. I feel the same.

DAVID

We all need somebody to talk to who
will give us honest feedback.

JESSICA

Yes, we do. David, we have one thing
in common for sure. We have both
experienced abuse. Your abuse is

psychological, whereas my abuse has been more physical. Both are terrible.

DAVID

I agree. They are certainly terrible! Let's start meeting for a drink on Fridays after work. We can talk and help each other with our problems.

JESSICA

(smiling)

Yes, let's do it.

Lights off.

<u>Scene 7</u>

Lights rise. The phone rings, and Carol answers it.

CAROL

Hello.

(pause)

Betty, of course you can come over for coffee.

(pause)

10:00 a.m. will be fine. I look forward to seeing you.

(pause)

Bye, Betty.

Lights off.

<u>Scene 8</u>

Lights rise. Betty and Carol are sitting in the living room.

CAROL

Betty, you look worried. Is everything all right?

BETTY

I have to tell you something. My husband told me not to tell you, but—

CAROL

(interrupting)

Tell me. Whatever it is, just please tell me. I am nervous. I need to know.

BETTY

My husband goes for drinks every Friday after work. He sees a young and attractive woman with—

CAROL

(interrupting)

My husband, correct?

BETTY

She is with David. My husband says they smile and laugh a lot and seem to really enjoy being around each other. I though you should know about it.

Carol stands up and starts pacing back and forth.

CAROL

(screaming)

I knew it! I always suspected that David was having an affair with one of those bimbos who works with him. I believe you, Betty, but I need to see this for myself. Tell me the name of the place where they meet.

Lights off.

<u>Scene 9</u>

Lights rise. David and Jessica are sitting in a booth at a bar.

30

DAVID

Jessica, you won't believe what I am
about to tell you.

JESSICA

Tell me.

DAVID

I don't have to read your lips
anymore. I can hear you!

JESSICA

When did you regain your hearing?

DAVID

Literally in the last minute. The
psychiatrist was right. He said if I
could relax, talk to a close friend, and
learn to read their lips, then my
hearing might return.

JESSICA

David, you are such a good man. I am
glad you can hear again.

DAVID

Thank you, but I feel guilty. My purpose was to help you, but I think I am getting more out of this than you are.

Jessica puts her hand on David's arm.

JESSICA

Oh, David! You don't realize how much you have helped me. Even though you have only been able to read my lips and cannot hear my tone of voice, you have been so helpful and understanding.

Carol walks to the booth where David and Jessica are seated.

CAROL

(screaming)

Damn you, David! I knew you were having an affair! You are not only unfaithful and a philanderer, but you acted like you were deaf around me so you would not have to listen to me. You are deceptive and a liar. I

was sitting over there in a corner
watching you blab a mile a minute.
You can hear her without looking at
her. Don't tell me you are deaf!

DAVID

It is not what you think. I can explain.

JESSICA

Madam, we are not having an affair.
David is helping me with some
personal issues. Please believe me. I
am going to leave now. You two need
to talk alone.

Jessica leaves the bar.

CAROL

(staring at David)

I will see you at home.

Lights off.

Scene 10

*Lights rise. David and Carol are sitting in their
living room.*

CAROL

(screaming)

I just knew I was right! You are a rat from the filthiest of sewers. You are the worst excuse for a human being I have ever known. I wish you were dead.

VOICE OF DAVID

I cannot hear what she is saying, but it must be bad, according to the expression on her face.

Lights off.

Act III

<u>Scene 1</u>

Lights rise. David is at the psychiatrist's office.

PSYCHIATRIST

Continue telling me what happened.

DAVID

I was talking to my friend Jessica last Friday after work, and my ability to hear returned. All of a sudden, Carol came to the booth where we were seated, and she went into an emotional tirade accusing us of doing all kinds of ridiculous and absurd things. I felt terrible, embarrassed, and full of rage. I started to stand up with my fists clenched, but all at once, I was deaf again.

PSYCHIATRIST

I will speak slowly so you can read my lips accurately. It is important that you know more about what is causing your condition.

DAVID

Thank you, Doctor.

PSYCHIATRIST

From what I can determine, the stress from your home life has been overwhelming for years.

DAVID

It has become even worse. I have had thoughts of getting a gun and—

PSYCHIATRIST

(interrupting)

David, let me stop you there. Your condition is indeed serious. However, as long as your deafness persists, you will probably not act on your aggressive impulses.

DAVID

They still scare me sometimes.

PSYCHIATRIST

David, that is not uncommon in situations such as yours. Let me explain your problem in more detail.

DAVID

Yes, please do. I need to know.

PSYCHIATRIST

We psychiatrists call your problem a
conversion hysterical neurosis. This
occurs when an individual's
overwhelming stress is converted
into a physical symptom, but in the
absence of any underlying pathology.

DAVID

Doctor, would you elaborate on that?

PSYCHIATRIST

In simpler terms, this means you do
not have a medical disease. There is
no breakdown or damage in the
structure of your ears that has caused
this malfunction. We call this
psychological deafness.

DAVID

Oh, but—

PSYCHIATRIST

(interrupting)

Patients like you frequently think that the problem is in their ears, but, in fact, the problem is in their minds. Therefore, recovery from this problem involves treating the mind.

DAVID

Can you tell me how the mind could do this?

PSYCHIATRIST

Certainly, David. The overwhelming stress that you are experiencing disturbs the delicate chemical balance in your brain and nervous system.

DAVID

The balance in my brain? I do not understand.

PSYCHIATRIST

Your neuropathways are blocked due to this imbalance—

                    DAVID

                (interrupting)

I think I understand! My mind is
attempting to relieve me from all
this—

                PSYCHIATRIST

                (interrupting)

Yes, you are right, David! Your mind is
attempting to relieve you of all the
mental anguish you have been
suffering from.

                    DAVID

So this is the cause for my deafness.
It makes sense to me. I am deaf when
I am around my wife. The deafness
relaxes me. I don't feel rage toward
her.

                PSYCHIATRIST

That is how it usually works. In your
case, your brain produced this
hysterical symptom because you
were being bombarded with sounds
that were very distressing to you.

DAVID

So my mind conveniently closed the
door to all sounds.

PSYCHIATRIST

(smiling)

Yes, that is what happened. You don't
need a surgeon to operate on your
ear. You need to find a way to
eliminate the stress in your life.

DAVID

So you are saying this psychological
deafness has been helpful to me.

(whispering)

Had I not gone deaf, I might have
acted on my aggressive impulses and
killed my wife.

PSYCHIATRIST

Yes, David.

DAVID

This deafness has kept me from going
to prison.

PSYCHIATRIST

(smiling)

You could say that. At times, your mind can be your worst enemy. At other times, it can be your best friend. David, you are gaining insight into the nature of your problems. You are becoming more aware.

DAVID

I am aware of the reasons for my problems, but this has not worked for me. In spite of my insight, I still hate my wife, and my deafness comes and goes. When my deafness does go away, I suffer so much that I am afraid I will kill my wife. What can I do about this, Doctor?

PSYCHIATRIST

I will tell you about your therapeutic options.

DAVID

I am ready; go ahead.

You can divorce your wife, you can continue therapy for an extended period of time, or you can just decide to live with the problem.

DAVID

I understand. If I choose to live with this psychological deafness, then I will get some relief, but maybe I should...I just don't know what to do.

PSYCHIATRIST

David, let me reiterate what we both know. This anguish and hatred is causing your hysteria, which is your psychological deafness. If you cannot rid yourself of such destructive emotions, you are not going to get better. That is why I suggested the option of getting a divorce.

DAVID

I just don't know what to do. My religion does not believe in divorce.

Lights off.

<u>Scene 2</u>

Lights on. David and Carol are in the living room of their home.

DAVID

Carol, I am going to pick up the mail.

David walks out of the house and then suddenly stops.

DAVID

(speaking to himself)

I feel relaxed, even happy! I can hear children playing and dogs barking. My God! I can hear again. This is wonderful!

David walks back into the house and hears Carol's voice.

CAROL

(angrily)

Damn you, David! What took you so long?

David looks closely at Carol. Her mouth is moving quickly, but he cannot hear anything. He smiles, looks at the mail, and then begins to whistle.

Lights slowly dim.

The Daughter

CHARACTERS

JEAN—twenty-year-old woman

SUSAN—fifty-year-old woman, Jean's adoptive mother

MAN—forty-year-old man, boyfriend of Evelyn

EVELYN—thirty-eight-year-old woman, Jean's birth mother

CHAUFFER—seventy-year-old man

PSYCHIATRIST—sixty-year-old man

YOUNG BLOND GIRL-18 year old

LOCATION

Los Angeles, California

TIME

2010

ACT I

<u>Scene 1</u>

Lights rise. A mother and daughter are sitting in the living room of their home.

JEAN

Mom, I love the internet!

SUSAN

I wish I knew how to use it.

JEAN

Sit next to me, and I will show you. I can find anything you want.

SUSAN

Anything?

JEAN

Yes. Mom, practically anything. I have actually been looking for information about my birth mother. What can you tell me about her?

SUSAN

Even though I saw her only briefly, I could tell she was a beautiful young lady. But, darling, so many years have gone by, you need to be careful because people change. She may not be in an emotional state to see you.

JEAN

I understand, Mom, but I really want to meet you. I have dreamed many times about a blond lady who looked like me. What color were her eyes?

SUSAN

They were blue. Her complexion was fair, and she had rosy cheeks.

JEAN

Tell me more about her.

SUSAN

Her eyes were very blue, and she had long eyelashes. Her blond hair had waves that fell down over her shoulders. I cried when she handed you over to me. She told me to take good care of you. I will never forget that moment. She knew in her heart that I would be the best mother for her. Do you really feel like you need to do this?

JEAN

Yes, Mom, I do. I have more questions about how she looked. Was she fat or skinny?

SUSAN

I don't know because she was wearing a hospital gown.

JEAN

I have been curious about her for a long time.

SUSAN

You were born in a hospital in a very small town not too far from here, but the hospital has closed. I don't know if you will be able to find the records.

Lights off.

<u>Scene 2</u>

Lights on.

JEAN

Mom, you are not going to believe it! I did some research, and the hospital where I was born is closed, but their records were transferred to the hospital here in town.

SUSAN

That is great news! You wanted to find out about the beautiful lady who gave birth to you. Go and find out, if you must.

Jean gives her mom a kiss on the cheek.

JEAN

Thank you, Mom.

Lights off.

<u>Scene 3</u>

Lights on. Jean is standing outside a house in a dilapidated neighborhood.

JEAN

(talking to herself)

I wonder if I have the correct address.

Jean looks at her cell phone.

JEAN

Yes, I do. This must be it.

Jean knocks on the door. A man answers the door.
He is dirty, unshaven, and missing his front
toothless, and he reeks of alcohol.

MAN

What do you want?

JEAN

May I please speak with Evelyn?

MAN

Come on in.

The man turns around and hollers toward Evelyn.

MAN

Evelyn, get your ass over here.
Someone wants to see you.

A haggard looking woman slowly enters the stage. She is wearing a filthy apron. Some of her front teeth are missing. There are bags under her blue eyes. The woman starts to wobble and appears to be drunk.

Jean suddenly goes blind.

JEAN

(screaming frantically)

Help me! Help me! I cannot see.

Jean stumbles around trying to find an exit. Evelyn takes her by the arm, leads her to the front door, and shouts to the chauffeur parked outside.

EVELYN

Come here and get this woman, whoever in the hell she is.

Lights off.

<u>Scene 4</u>

Lights on. Jean, visibly upset, arrives back at her home. The chauffeur helps her to the front door. Her mother opens the door.

52

SUSAN

Are you OK?

JEAN

(crying)

No, Mom. I cannot see. I am blind!

Susan takes Jean by the arm, and they sit in the living room.

SUSAN

(caressing Jean's hair)

What happened? Did someone hit you?

JEAN

No, Mom. All I can remember is a rough-looking man opening a door and taking me into his living room. Then I heard him yell, "Evelyn, get in here!" I vaguely remember the image of a woman coming into the room, and then I went blind.

(She cries).

Mom, I did not hit my head on anything or fall down. I just don't know what happened other than I just went blind.

Lights off.

<u>Scene 5</u>

Lights on. Jean and Susan are at the psychiatrist's office.

SUSAN

That is all I can tell you, Doctor. Jean told me exactly the same thing when she arrived home. She did not hit her head before she went blind or during the instant when she saw her birth mother.

The psychiatrist checks Jean's vital signs.

PSYCHIATRIST

Jean, this is clearly a psychological problem. There is absolutely nothing physiologically wrong with your brain that would cause you to go blind. Also, the sensory receptors in your brain that enable you to see have no structural damage.

JEAN

Then what is causing it?

PSYCHIATRIST

You are suffering from a conversion hysterical reaction.

JEAN

What is that, and what causes it?

PSYCHIATRIST

Extreme and sudden stress.

JEAN

That would cause me to go blind?

PSYCHIATRIST

Yes. Extreme and sudden stress is converted into a physical symptom with no underlying pathology. Your primary physician was right. This is purely a psychological problem. When I say no underlying pathology, it means there is no physical disease that led to your blindness.

JEAN

(holding back tears)

Why did this happen to me?

PSYCHIATRIST

To find the source of the problem, I need to know what you have been going through for the last several weeks.

JEAN

I have been searching for my birth mother. I went to the house where I thought she lived. I saw a woman for just a split second, and then I went blind.

PSYCHIATRIST

Tell me, Jean. What did you expect your mother to physically look like? Did you expect her to look cultured, like the woman who adopted you? What did you expect her general behavior to be?

JEAN

My adoptive mother told me that my birth mother was beautiful and, I assumed, sophisticated also.

PSYCHIATRIST

Jean, based on what you told me about the man who answered the door at your birth mother's house and invited you in, it was stressful for you. This was compounded by your visual perception of how terribly kept the house was and the conditions in general. Also, the physical appearance of the man and his lack of any sophistication was surely very upsetting to you. This added to the stress that you were experiencing. Everything that you saw was dramatically opposite of what you expected.

JEAN

(crying and speaking in a low voice)

Yes, Doctor, that does make sense to me.

PSYCHIATRIST

The woman who entered the living room was probably not attractive and, perhaps, totally unsophisticated.

JEAN

But even if what you said is correct, I still do not understand why I went blind.

PSYCHIATRIST

I will explain it to you. When your birth mother came into the living room, your eyes took a very quick picture of the image. Think of it as a camera taking a photograph. Your eyes saw something that your mind could not handle. It could not accept the image at that given point in time. The stress was overwhelming. What you saw in an imperceptible unit of time was very threatening to you. It was not what your mind expected, so your mind engaged in what we call ego-defensive behavior. It converted the stress into a physical symptom, your blindness. Your brain did not

want to see what was in front of you,
so it had no recourse other than to
temporarily take away your sight.

JEAN

How did going blind help me?

PSYCHIATRIST

Had you not gone blind, you might
have had a nervous breakdown or
gone into a severe state of
depression and even become suicidal.
Jean, it may be that your blindness
saved your life. Your brain wants you
to live.

JEAN

Doctor, I don't want to stay blind for
the remainder of my life!

PSYCHIATRIST

Don't worry. You will not. In cases
like this, the blindness, the symptom,
will go away with the passage of
time. However, therapy could make
the blindness disappear more rapidly.

JEAN

Doctor, I am sorry, but could you repeat what happened to me? This is all so overwhelming. If I could understand it better, I think that would really help me.

PSYCHIATRIST

Of course, Jean. You saw something dreadful. The stress was overwhelming and disrupted the delicate chemical balance in your brain.

JEAN

Please continue.

PSYCHIATRIST

This caused a buildup of a certain chemical agent that blocked the pathways of the sensory neurons responsible for producing sight. Let me put it another way. Jean, imagine you are in a dental office to get a tooth pulled. The dentist gives you a shot to deaden the nerves responsible for sending messages to your tooth and the tissue surrounding your tooth. This is done so you will not feel pain and suffer.

JEAN

It is not as complicated as I thought.

PSYCHIATRIST

Would you agree to come once a week for therapy? I can help you.

JEAN

Yes, Doctor. I want to get well.

Act II

<u>Scene 1</u>

Lights on. Jean is at the psychiatrist's office.

> PSYCHIATRIST

Jean, we have had many therapeutic sessions. Could you please tell me what you have learned?

> JEAN

Yes, Doctor. I expected my mother to have culture, to be attractive and sophisticated.

> PSYCHIATRIST

And…

> JEAN

And until I can accept her for who she really is rather than who I expected her to be, the therapy will not be successful.

> PSYCHIATRIST

Anything else?

62

JEAN

Yes, Doctor. Now I have an
awareness of the conditions that
made my mother who she is now.

PSYCHIATRIST

Is that enough for you?

JEAN

No, because my psychological barrier
to recovery will not be eliminated
until I focus more on my mother and
less on myself.

PSYCHIATRIST

Very good, Jean!

JEAN

As you said, I must emotionally
change my overall attitude toward
my mother and focus on two things:
unconditional love and acceptance.

PSYCHIATRIST

Jean, there is not much more I can do
for you unless you are willing to meet
with your birth mother in my office. It

is going to take one-on-one contact with her in order for you to recover and regain your sight. Are you willing to go through this?

JEAN

Yes, Doctor, but I am not sure that my birth mother would be willing to participate.

PSYCHIATRIST

Why don't you ask your adoptive mother to go to your birth mother's house and explain what has happened to you. She can explain to her that you may not recover without her help.

Lights off.

<u>Scene 2</u>

Lights on. Susan knocks on Evelyn's door. Evelyn is shabbily dressed and looks beaten down.

EVELYN

Lady, I don't know who the hell you are, but you are at the wrong house. No one comes to this neighborhood well dressed and driving an expensive car.

Evelyn starts to close the door.

SUSAN

No, please don't close the door. I am the woman who adopted your daughter twenty years ago. I remember your name. You are Evelyn.

EVELYN

(speaking in a subdued and sad tone of voice)

OK, what do you want from me now?

SUSAN

Your daughter, Jean, has gone blind. Her psychiatrist says that she may not recover without your help. You may remember her. She visited you recently.

EVELYN

There was a young lady who came by the house a few weeks ago. My boyfriend let her in.

SUSAN

Yes, that was Jean.

EVELYN

He called me into the living room, but before I could ask her what she wanted, she started screaming that she needed help because she was blind. My boyfriend thought she was crazy or under the influence of something. I walked her to the front porch, where an older man was waiting for her. He helped her to the car, and they drove away. Lady, my boyfriend is gone, so we can talk alone. Please come in.

Susan enters the house and sits down.

EVELYN

Tell me something. Was that young woman really my daughter?

SUSAN

Yes, Evelyn. There is no doubt. We conducted a thorough investigation,

and I am sure of it. Is your maiden
name Brown?

SUSAN EVELYN

(in a soft voice)

Yes. I have to admit that I have been
very sad over the years thinking
about giving her up for adoption. I
had...well, I still have a drinking
problem.

SUSAN

When did it start?

EVELYN

It started about a month after I gave
birth.

SUSAN

Did you have a job at that time?

EVELYN

I did before I got pregnant. I had a bit
part in a movie. I was able to provide
for myself, but with the alcohol
abuse...

(she starts to cry.)

As you can see, I just went downhill,
and then I hit rock bottom.

SUSAN

What about the father? Didn't he
want to help you in any way?

EVELYN

No! Not at all! He was married. When
I told him that I was pregnant with his
child, he denied paternity and told
me that I would be blackballed from
the industry if I spoke up about the
affair. He promised he would make
me a movie star, but as you can
plainly see, that did not happen.

SUSAN

If you want, we can do something
about your problem with alcohol. I
have the resources and contacts to
help you, but will you keep quiet the
details of the birth?

EVELYN

I will take that secret to my grave.
(sobbing) Thank you. I need help. I

am glad my boyfriend is not here. I am ashamed that I ever got involved with someone like him. I wish you could have known me when I was young. I thought I was going to be the next big star.

SUSAN

Evelyn, we all make mistakes, but back to Jean. Jean's doctor would like for you to come to his office. I will be there with Jean. The doctor believes that it will take all three of us in a group setting to assist in Jean's recovery.

EVELYN

I want to help my little girl. I gave her life, but I never gave her anything else. If I say no, I would not be able to live with myself.

SUSAN

Thank you so much. I will come by twice a week and take you to the doctor's office.

Lights off.

<u>Scene 3</u>

Lights on. Susan and Jean are at home.

SUSAN

Honey, I need to speak with you about something. I went by your birth mother's house. We need her help so you can get well. I hope you are not mad at me.

JEAN

(hugging Susan)

No, Mom, not all. I am grateful. I want to get well. I will do whatever it takes.

SUSAN

I had a long talk with her. She was very sad about everything. She agreed to meet with the doctor and us for as long as it takes for you to get better.

JEAN

I am so glad.

SUSAN

She is living in poverty and has a
drinking problem.

JEAN

How old is she?

SUSAN

She is only thirty-eight, but she looks
fifty-eight. Jean, I know this is going
to be difficult for you, but your
recovery depends on it. You will also
be doing a great service for your birth
mother. In fact, this may emotionally
save her life. She is so self-destructive
that she is either emotionally beating
up on herself or getting drunk. I hope
we can trust her.

JEAN

I agree with you. Let's help her. We
can all support one another.

Lights off.

<u>Scene 4</u>

*Lights on. Evelyn, Jean and Susan are sitting in the
waiting room of the psychiatrist's office.*

EVELYN

(sadly)

Susan, I never meant to hurt my babies.

JEAN

Mom, did she say babies?

SUSAN

(standing up)

Enough of this! Let's go home.

Evelyn tries to hold Susan by the arm.

EVELYN

Wait! Wait! I was young and naïve. I had dreams that Jean and Jimmy would have held me back.

JEAN

Jimmy? Who was Jimmy? Are you saying that I have a brother?

SUSAN

Be quiet, Evelyn! You don't know what you are talking about. Stop with your malicious lies! Just go back to your filthy house.

Susan grabs Jean by the arm.

Come with me, Jean. We are leaving now.

Light shines on the corner of the stage. A young blond girl is talking to herself and holding a baby in a blue blanket.

YOUNG BLOND GIRL

I cannot believe she did not want my baby boy. She took only the girl. *(She kisses the baby in the blanket)* You were so little.

She puts her baby down and takes a liquor bottle and a newspaper out of her bag. She reads the newspaper headline aloud.

Local Woman Acquitted of Charges. Son's Death Ruled Accidental.

YOUNG BLOND GIRL

(screaming)

It was an accident! I drank too much and brought you to bed with me because you would not stop crying.

Believe me, my little Jimmy, I did not kill you. I loved you when nobody else wanted you. It truly was an accident. You were only one month old and I was drunk. When I finally woke up, you were quiet and your little body was cold.

Lights off.

<u>Scene 5</u>

Lights on. Susan, Evelyn, and Jean are having lunch at a restaurant months later.

SUSAN

Evelyn, I must tell you how pretty you look!

EVELYN

Thank you. I am grateful for the positive changes in my life. I am going to AA, and I get to spend time with my daughter. I am happy for the first time in years.

JEAN

(holding up her water glass)

A toast to my two moms and my twin brother who is in heaven. Thank you both for everything. I love you so much. Spending time with you two has made me so happy and facilitated my recovery. I know our sessions with the doctor were not always pleasant, but I have never been happier. Not many people can say they have two great moms! It also feels good to see again! Also, a toast to my dad, a great movie director.

EVELYN

Susan, you were married to a movie director here in Los Angeles?

Susan looks at Evelyn straight in the eye.

SUSAN

Yes. He died a few years ago but he was dead to me when I found out he had an affair with an aspiring young actress. *(sarcastically)* Rest in peace.

Lights low.

SUSAN

(walking away and talking to herself)

She took away my happy life, but I raised her daughter. One can say that we are even.

Lights slowly dim.

The Soldier

Characters

FATHER—fifty-year-old man, father of Konrad

KONRAD—twenty-four-year-old man

FIRST SERGEANT—thirty-year-old man

OLDER VETERAN SERGEANT—fifty-year-old man

COMMANDER—sixty-year-old man

MEDIC—twenty-year-old man

PSYCHIATRIST—sixty-year-old man

MOTHER—forty-seven-year-old woman, mother of Konrad

VETERAN #1—man in his fifties

VETERAN #2—man in his fifties

VETERAN #3—man in his fifties

LOCATION

Peoria, Illinois

TIME

Late 1940s and early 1950s

Act I

<u>Scene 1</u>

Lights on. Two people are sitting at the kitchen table.

FATHER

Konrad, my son, do you realize that in thirty days, you will be entering the greatest military school in the world?

KONRAD

Yes, Dad. I am glad that I was accepted at the West Point Military Academy.

FATHER

Some of the greatest generals in the United States Army graduated from that fine institution. Just to name a few, Ulysses S. Grant—

KONRAD

(interrupting)

I remember him. He eventually became president, correct?

FATHER

Yes, and he served in the Civil War as commander in chief of the Northern army. Do you remember me telling you about Robert E. Lee? I told you stories about him when you were young.

KONRAD

I do remember. You told me he was commander in chief of the Southern army. You also said that, in your opinion, he was the greatest general in the history of the country.

FATHER

Yes, I remember saying that, and I still believe it. Dwight D. Eisenhower also went to West Point. He distinguished himself during World War II as a great strategist. He planned and orchestrated the invasion of Normandy, which led to the liberation of France and ultimately to the defeat of Nazi Germany.

KONRAD

I will probably study about him at
West Point.

FATHER

I am certain that you will. There were
many other great generals who
distinguished themselves in war, such
as General Black Jack Pershing,
General Douglas MacArthur, and
General George Patton.

KONRAD

Dad, I am glad our family has a proud
military tradition.

FATHER

Thank you, son. Our military tradition
is also very important to me. I served
in World War II, and your grandfather
was in World War I. My two great-
grandfathers also served this great
country of ours in time of war.

KONRAD

Which wars?

FATHER

The Spanish-American War and the
Civil War.

KONRAD

Dad, I studied about the Spanish-
American War. It was fought
between the United States and Spain
in 1898.

FATHER

Yes, son! Your great-grandfather
served with Teddy Roosevelt as they
attacked San Juan Hill. Roosevelt later
became president of the United
States.

KONRAD

Dad, tell me about the other great-
grandfather.

Military music plays in the background.

FATHER

He served during the Civil War on the
side of the North.

KONRAD

Under which general?

FATHER

General Grant. Your great-grandfather was badly wounded, but he survived and was decorated for valor.

KONRAD

Dad, tell me about your experiences in World War II. I used to ask you about them when I was a kid, but you would always say you would tell me some other time.

FATHER

I don't like to talk about myself.

KONRAD

Dad, I will be a soldier in thirty days. It is important for me to know about your experiences as a soldier.

FATHER

Well, probably my most vivid
memory is when my infantry platoon
was surrounded by a group of
Japanese soldiers on an island in the
South Pacific.

KONRAD

Where exactly did that happen?

FATHER

On an island called Iwo Jima. There
were hundreds or more Japanese
screaming, "Banzai, banzai!"

KONRAD

What does that mean?

FATHER

They were war cries. They were
preparing to attack us and slaughter
us all.

KONRAD

Were you scared?

FATHER

Of course I was scared. We were all
scared, but a soldier keeps on doing
his duty in spite of what looks like
certain death.

KONRAD

Were they far away from you?

FATHER

No, they were only fifty yards or so
away from us. As they started bearing
down on us, firing their weapons and
screaming like madmen, we opened
up on them with everything we had.

Sound of gunfire in the background.

KONRAD

That must have been like a living hell.

FATHER

I never felt so much fear in my life.
We were dug in pretty well, but
bullets were flying all around us.

KONRAD

What if you hadn't killed them?

FATHER

Well, they would have shot us, or
worse yet, they would have
bayoneted us to death. We all feared
that cold steel penetrating our
bodies.

KONRAD

Dad, did your pray?

FATHER

Yes! We were praying to God to help
us out. Son, there are no atheists in
foxholes.

KONRAD

(nodding his head)

I understand.

FATHER

The fear was so intense that I wanted
to run away. I even urinated in my
pants.

KONRAD

Oh, Dad!

FATHER

To make a long story short, we had
more firepower than they did.

KONRAD

Thank God!

FATHER

After ten minutes of ferocious
combat, ending in hand-to-hand
combat, the Japanese soldiers were
either all killed or badly wounded.
They just lay there dying.

KONRAD

What happened next?

FATHER

A few of the soldiers finished them
off. My son, I could not do that, but it
sometimes happens in war.

KONRAD

How many men were in your group?

FATHER

Forty. Out of the forty men in our platoon, ten were killed and twenty-one were wounded.

KONRAD

I remember seeing a medal among your war things in the attic.

FATHER

I was decorated and I was called a war hero, but I want to tell you right now that I almost ran away. Thank God that I did not. When all hell broke loose, I remember what an old-timer told me years ago. He said, "Cowards die a thousand times, but a hero dies but once."

KONRAD

I like that saying. I have never heard it before.

FATHER

Son, when I look back on it, I believe that my memory of that saying was the reason that I did not run away.

Whether or not I deserve to be called a hero I don't know, but I know that I was not a coward.

The father and Konrad hug each other.

Lights off.

Act II

<u>Scene 1</u>

Lights off. Music is playing in the background. Konrad's father and mother are waiting for Konrad after the graduation ceremony. Konrad walks onto the stage dressed in his military uniform. They hug their son.

> FATHER
>
> You made it, son! We are so proud of you! You have continued the military tradition of our family.

Konrad's mother leaves the stage.

> KONRAD
>
> Dad, I have some big news for you. I am joining the infantry, and I am proud of it.

> FATHER
>
> *(patting his son on the back)*
>
> That's my boy!

KONRAD

I am going to tell you something, Dad.
I will leave it up to you as to when we
tell Mom. I just received my orders. I
am being sent to Korea.

FATHER

Korea?

KONRAD

Yes, Dad. This is what I wanted. I
want to be the kind of brave soldier
that you, my grandfather, and my
great-grandfathers were.

The father hugs Konrad.

FATHER

I am even more proud of you. Go
over there and win some battles.
Honor your country, honor yourself,
and honor your entire family.

Lights off.

<u>Scene 2</u>

Lights on. Two months later. Konrad's parents are sitting in their living room reading a letter from him.

FATHER

(reading the letter aloud)

Dear Mom and Dad,

I hope you are well. Only two months have passed since I got here, but I have already been promoted to first lieutenant. I will be assigned to an infantry company as the company commander. My men and I have been through rigorous combat training. I am not certain when I will experience real combat, but it will be soon.

I love you, Mom and Dad.

Konrad

PS—Dad, I will fight with the same dedication that you did.

Lights off.

<u>Scene 3</u>

Lights on. Three weeks later in South Korea. Konrad is standing in front of the colonel of his battalion.

KONRAD

(salutes the colonel)

Sir, we need reinforcements to help hold our left flank. We are about to be overrun.

COLONEL

Lieutenant, we cannot provide you with any reinforcements. You must hold your position at all costs.

KONRAD

Yes, Colonel. We will give it all we have.

Later that day.

KONRAD

First Sergeant, our request was denied. There are no reinforcements available. Tell the men on the left flank that we have been ordered to hold the line at all costs. I will take care of the right flank.

Two hours later, the battle is over. They have held their positions. Konrad surveys the battlefield. Konrad addresses the leaders of each platoon.

KONRAD

Give me a body count. I want to know how many are dead and how many are wounded.

Konrad walks to the side of the stage.

KONRAD

(talking to himself)

Dad, I got through our first battle with only a slight leg wound. We held our ground. What got me through it all were the stories that you shared with me about your experiences as a combat soldier. Now I know how you felt with that overwhelming fear. Like you, Dad, I never gave in to my fear. Dad, I stood my ground. The impulse to run away was there, but I did not give in to it. Do you remember the statement about cowards dying a

thousand times? It gave me the
courage to perform my duties well.

Lights off.

<u>Scene 4</u>

Lights on.

FIRST SERGEANT

Lieutenant, sir!

KONRAD

Do you have the information I
requested?

FIRST SERGEANT

Yes. Fifty men killed and seventy-two
wounded.

KONRAD

Tell the men they did a damn good
job. I am going back to my position.

Konrad walks away limping.

FIRST SERGEANT

Lieutenant, your ankle is covered
with blood.

KONRAD

It is just a flesh wound. The medic will patch it up. Sergeant, tell all the platoon sergeants to meet me at 2100 hours.

Lights off.

<u>Scene 5</u>

Lights on. Konrad is speaking in front of the troops.

KONRAD

Can you all hear me?

The men respond affirmatively.

KONRAD

We are not going to get any relief. We move out tomorrow and join the Second Battalion near the Yalu River. They need reinforcements badly. The Chinese have crossed the river, and they are attacking our outposts in hordes. They have overrun several battalions on the outpost of the perimeter. Many American soldiers have been wounded and killed. God only knows how many have been captured.

OLDER VETERAN SERGEANT

Sir, I want to share something with you. The men in your company were leery of you because you had no prior combat experience, but you have won their respect.

KONRAD

Thank you for telling me that, Sergeant.

OLDER VETERAN SERGEANT

May I continue?

KONRAD

Yes.

OLDER VETERAN SERGEANT

When the medic was treating one of our wounded soldiers close to the enemy line, he was gunned down by the enemy. Several men in my platoon say you crawled out there with bullets flying all around, but you still dragged him to safety.

At the back of stage, a soldier is dragging another soldier while the sound of bullets can be heard.

OLDER VETERAN SERGEANT

They know you were wounded in the process. Lieutenant, when you do something like that, the men will follow you to hell and back.

Later that day.

Konrad is talking to his company.

KONRAD

Men, now that we have joined the Third Battalion, we are going to be involved in a bloody battle. In twenty-four hours, we have to take a hill called Bloody Ridge. It has that name because the First and Second Battalions were also almost completely wiped out there two months ago. They had no aerial support. Now the good news. The Air Force is going to bomb the hell out of the hill and soften it up. However, I have to tell you something. This is not going to be a Sunday-afternoon picnic. Some of us are not going to make it. Gentlemen, put your magazines in the bottom of your field packs, and put your Bible at the top.

The sounds of bullets and screams of wounded soldiers are heard in the background.

Twenty-four hours later.

FIRST SERGEANT

Lieutenant, we have taken the hill and driven off what was left of the enemy.

A battalion commander enters the stage.

COMMANDER

Lieutenant, I want to congratulate you and your men for a job well done. I understand we lost a lot of men and many men were wounded, but war is hell, and losing our freedom would be worse. Now that we have taken the hill, I have received orders to hold it.

Later that day.

FIRST SERGEANT

Lieutenant, will there be a counterattack?

KONRAD

Most likely, as the terrain will be in our favor. The enemy will have to come up the hill. We have the advantage this time because we will be at the top firing down on them. We also have the woods to shield us from the enemy's sight.

Now we are under the command of General Harper. He is the commander of the Twenty-Fourth Infantry Division. He is withdrawing companies A, C, and D from the battalion. So our company B, along with E Company, will have the burden of holding the hill.

(his voice cracking)

I saw a lot of good men go down...I wonder who is next. Did you know that Corporal White was killed?

FIRST SERGEANT

Yes, sir. I heard his head was blown
off.

KONRAD

He was only a few feet away from
me.

(He raises his right hand over his field jacket.)

His blood splattered all over me.

(He pauses and looks down.)

I am getting tired of ordering my men
to go into situations where I know
that some of them are going to get
killed.

*There are a few seconds of silence between the
two men. The first sergeant puts his hand on the
lieutenant's shoulder.*

FIRST SERGEANT

Sir, we will make it. Hell's fire, we are
too ornery to die.

KONRAD

Sergeant, do you have any whiskey
on you?

The sergeant reaches into his jacket and hands Konrad his flask.

                    FIRST SERGEANT

          Here you go, sir.

Two days later.

                         KONRAD

          We have been ordered to go on the
          offensive against the enemy before
          they can attack us. Let's do it.

As the troops move forward, the sound of enemy mortar fire is deafening.

                    FIRST SERGEANT

          Sir, the firepower has let up
          somewhat. Should we advance
          forward again?

Lieutenant Konrad attempts to stand up, but he cannot move his legs.

                    FIRST SERGEANT

          Sir, what the hell is wrong with you?
          We better get moving.

KONRAD

I can't move my damn legs.

FIRST SERGEANT

Medic! Medic! Bring a litter here and evacuate the lieutenant.

The medics put him on the litter.

MEDIC

Sir, where were you hit?

KONRAD

I was not hit. I just can't move my legs.

Lights off.

Act III

<u>Scene 1</u>

Lights on. Lieutenant Konrad and a psychiatrist are talking at a medical facility away from the battlefield.

PSYCHIATRIST

Lieutenant, your legs are paralyzed.

KONRAD

Doc, how could that be? I have not even been wounded.

PSYCHIATRIST

It is a psychological problem. To be more specific, a neurological problem. I have seen several cases like this over the past year.

KONRAD

Why? What causes this?

PSYCHIATRIST

It usually happens to men who have experienced high levels of stress in combat situations over a period of time.

KONRAD

Yes, I have been feeling a lot of
stress—

PSYCHIATRIST

(interrupting)

Lieutenant, your mind felt that it had
to do something to relieve you of all
this overwhelming stress. With your
legs paralyzed, you could not walk.
Therefore, you could not go into
battle and experience the stress that
battle causes.

KONRAD

But how and why did this happen? I
still don't understand.

PSYCHIATRIST

You were in an approach-avoidance
conflict. You wanted to approach the
battle zone—

KONRAD

(interrupting)

Yes, it was my duty. I owed it to my
men, and I did not want to be seen as
a coward.

PSYCHIATRIST

Exactly. You wanted to avoid the
battle zone because you did not want
to be killed.

KONRAD

Yes! Yes! I did not want to die. I
wanted to be with my family.

PSYCHIATRIST

You also wanted to avoid the
horrifying feeling that fear produces.

KONRAD

Yes. I hate to admit it, but you are
right.

PSYCHIATRIST

You developed a conversion
hysterical disorder that gave you a
legitimate out from the terrible

situations that you were experiencing.

KONRAD

(in an aggressive and defensive tone)

Doc, I am not a chicken! No way would I engage in a cowardly act!

(holding back tears)

You have to believe me!

PSYCHIATRIST

You did not engage in any kind of cowardly act! Listen to me! You did not consciously will your legs to be paralyzed. You did not retreat from battle. You did not run away. Lieutenant, think of it this way. Because your legs were paralyzed, in a way, you were like a wounded soldier with his legs blown off. Soldiers cannot perform their duties without legs.

KONRAD

Yes...

PSYCHIATRIST

With your condition, leg paralysis, it is impossible to walk.

KONRAD

I understand, but...

PSYCHIATRIST

Lieutenant, you are a well-educated man, so let me explain in greater detail what happened to you neurologically. The overwhelming stress disturbed the delicate chemical balance in your nervous system.

KONRAD

I am beginning to understand it better.

PSYCHIATRIST

Good! This caused the neural pathway leading to the effectors and motor nerves to be blocked.

KONRAD

So the message to my leg muscles—

PSYCHIATRIST

(interrupting)

Correct. The message to contract your leg muscles does not get through.

Lights off.

<u>Scene 2</u>

Lights on. Two months later in a military hospital in California. Konrad's parents enter the stage to see Konrad walking back and forth.

FATHER

Son, it is so good to see you!

Konrad hugs his parents.

KONRAD

It is good to see you, Mom and Dad.

FATHER

Good! You are walking around. Which leg—or was it both legs that were wounded?

KONRAD

Neither one, Dad. According to the psychiatrist, my legs became paralyzed because of prolonged combat fatigue.

FATHER

(speaking in a loud and offensive tone)

No matter how tired a young man's legs get, he can still walk!

KONRAD

But, Dad—

FATHER

(interrupting)

Be quiet! You copped out. You dishonored your fellow soldiers, our family, and our family history of brave young men going all the way back to the Civil War.

MOTHER

Jim, please stop it. Can't you see how upset and sorry he is about what happened to him?

FATHER

(screaming)

I don't give a damn what happened to him! Do you know what he is?

MOTHER

Yes, I know what he is. He is a good man.

FATHER

(screaming)

No, he is a coward and a disgrace to the military and our family military tradition.

Konrad's father takes his wife by the arm and hurries out of the hospital room. Before they leave, the hospital psychiatrist stops them.

PSYCHIATRIST

Would you please come with me to my office? I want to explain Konrad's condition and what he is going through.

FATHER

(speaking in a loud and angry tone)

I don't want to talk to any shrink. All you do is make up excuses for weak people.

Six months later. The war is over, and Konrad is discharged from the military.

Lights off.

Act IV

<u>Scene 1</u>

Lights on. Konrad knocks at the front door of his parents' home. Nobody answers, so he sits on their front porch and starts talking to himself.

KONRAD

I received a Bronze and Silver Star for heroism in two major battles. I am proud that I served my country honorably and heroically. When Dad comes home, I hope to find out that he has changed his mind about my military service.

Konrad's mother arrives home. She hugs Konrad.

MOTHER

Konrad! Thank God you are home.

KONRAD

Mom, it is so good to be home. Where is Dad?

MOTHER

He will be home any minute now. He will be happy to see you.

KONRAD

I hope so.

Konrad's father enters the stage.

KONRAD

Dad, great to see you! I am glad to be home with you and Mom.

Konrad tries to hug his father, but his father backs away and only offers to shake his hand.

FATHER

(in an emotionless tone of voice)

I am glad you are home.

KONRAD

Thank you, Dad. Well, Mom and Dad, I am going to bed. It was a long trip from California. Let's catch up on things tomorrow. Good night.

Lights off.

<u>Scene 2</u>

Lights on. Konrad's father is reading the newspaper and drinking a cup of coffee at the kitchen table. Konrad enters the room.

KONRAD

Good morning, Dad.

FATHER

Sit down. From what I have read in the local newspaper, you distinguished yourself as a soldier. I was wrong. You have honored your family tradition by being a brave and good soldier.

KONRAD

Thanks, Dad.

FATHER

I have to excuse myself. I need to go to the VFW. We are discussing future events for soldiers returning from the war.

MOTHER

Dad, don't forget! We are meeting at Schneithorst's restaurant at 4:00 p.m. to celebrate Konrad's homecoming.

The father stands up and starts to leave without looking at either of them.

FATHER

See you.

Lights off.

<u>Scene 3</u>

Lights rise. Konrad's father and a few veterans are standing at the bar at the VFW.

VETERAN #1

Hey, Jim, come here and sit down. We are ready to start the meeting.

VETERAN #2

Jim, we all read about your son.

VETERAN #3

I bet you are so proud of him. Being awarded the Silver Star and the Bronze Star is really something to be proud of.

FATHER

Oh, yes. I am proud of my boy!

The veterans stand up and raise their beer mugs.

VETERAN #1

Let's all toast to Jim's son. He is a war
hero.

*The father leaves the VFW and starts speaking to
himself.*

FATHER

I can't believe the way I treated my
son at the military hospital and then
again yesterday. I am ashamed of
myself. What I did was just plain
stupid. He is going to be home for a
while, and I am going to spend all my
time trying to make up for my
stupidity.

*The father arrives at the restaurant dressed in his
World War II military uniform. He joins his family
and friends at their table.*

FATHER

(smiling)

Son, your father, a World War II
veteran, salutes you.

*Konrad's father gives his son a military salute and
then hugs him.*

KONRAD

Thanks, Dad.

FATHER

Son, I am so damn proud of you! I don't think that I would have had the guts to do what you did on the battlefield.

Konrad and his father hug again.

KONRAD

Thank you, Dad. I love you, and I respect you.

A reporter takes a picture of the two men in uniform.

Lights slowly dim.

The Painter

CHARACTERS

JEFF—early thirties, son of Agnes

VICTORIA—mid-twenties, Jeff's girlfriend

MOTHER—late sixties, Jeff's mother

AUNT ESTHER—early sixties, Jeff's aunt

MINISTER—early forties

DR. BLOOMFIELD—late fifties, family doctor

DR. BROWN—late sixties, psychiatrist

LOCATION

San Francisco, California

TIME

2010

Act I

<u>Scene 1</u>

Lights on. Jeff is sitting at the dining room table eating breakfast with his mother and aunt.

AUNT ESTHER

Jeff, call off your wedding. I beg you. You will get over Victoria in no time.

MOTHER

I have heard that Victoria is not a very nice person, and her morals—

AUNT ESTHER

(interrupting)

Her morals are very loose.

MOTHER

Yes! She is from a good family, but—

AUNT ESTHER

(interrupting)

But she is the black sheep of her family.

Jeff stands up and throws his napkin on the table.

JEFF

(angrily)

Stop it! You do the same with all my girlfriends. Do you remember Melody? She was not good enough for me. Do you remember Alice and Martha? They were not well educated. Let's not forget Andrea. She was the nicest, kindest, and most polite woman I have ever met, but she did not live in the right neighborhood.

AUNT ESTHER

We just want the best for you.

MOTHER

Please, son, it is not too late to reconsider marrying Victoria.

JEFF

(full of anger)

Mom and Auntie, stop it! I am going to marry Victoria, and that is that!

Jeff knocks over a chair as he leaves the table. He tries to pick it up, but his hands are trembling so

*badly that he just kicks it aside. He leaves the
room.*

MOTHER

Sister, what can we do? The wedding
is tomorrow.

AUNT ESTHER

Have you told Jeff that you will
disinherit him if he marries Victoria?

MOTHER

Yes, many times, but he told me that
he didn't care. He said his paintings
were selling for a lot of money, and
he does not need an inheritance.

AUNT ESTHER

Do we have to accept her?

MOTHER

(screaming)

I will never accept her. I prefer to lose
my son.

AUNT ESTHER

(screaming)

Don't you dare say that again!

MOTHER

I will say it again and again. I would rather lose my son than have him marry that woman.

Lights off.

Later that day.

Lights on. Jeff is walking around the stage.

JEFF

(speaking to himself)

Victoria is a good woman. We understand each other. I cannot wait to be alone with her. I feel like I am in war zone when I am at my mom's house. The threats and arguments are wearing me down. I can feel relaxed only when I am with Victoria. She is a calm person. I am glad that I will marry her tomorrow. I better get some rest. It is late, and I want to be fresh for the wedding.

Lights off.

<u>Scene 2</u>

Lights on. Jeff and Victoria are getting married at a church. Jeff's best man hands him a ring. Victoria extends her left hand toward Jeff. He drops the ring. The best man picks it up and hands it back to Jeff, but Jeff cannot grasp it. His fingers and hands are paralyzed.

MINISTER

> Jeff, put the ring on your bride's finger.

Jeff, looking extremely upset, turns around and hurries out of the church. His mother and Aunt Esther look at each other in amazement. Victoria picks up the ring and watches Jeff leave the church. She is astonished at what has happened. She walks out of the church. Jeff's mother and Aunt Esther slowly leave the church smiling.

MOTHER

(whispering)

> Sister, we won!

Lights off.

ACT II

<u>Scene 1</u>

Lights on. Jeff is sitting in the office of the family doctor, Dr. Bloomfield.

DR. BLOOMFIELD

Hello, Jeff. How are you? How are your mom and aunt doing?

JEFF

They are fine, Doctor. I am the one with the problem.

DR. BLOOMFIELD

Tell me what it is.

JEFF

(holds out his hands)

Doctor, I cannot move my hands. They seem to be paralyzed.

DR. BLOOMFIELD

(examining Jeff's hands)

Let me see. Have you ever experienced this problem before?

JEFF

No, never.

DR. BLOOMFIELD

Jeff, I cannot find anything physically
wrong. I think your problem is
psychological.

JEFF

Psychological? What am I going to
do? I need my hands not only for
everyday life, but they are also how I
make a living. I am an artist, and I
need to prepare for my next art
exhibit.

DR. BLOOMFIELD

I know. I read about your one-man
show. Tell me something: Did you
feel stress before you lost your ability
to use your hands?

JEFF

Yes, I certainly did, but my main
concern now is to regain the use of
my hands as soon as possible.

DR. BLOOMFIELD

I am not a psychiatrist, but I know a good one, and I think you should see him. His name is Dr. Brown, and he is a psychiatrist and a neurologist. He will be able to diagnose and treat your problem.

Later that day.

Jeff is sitting in Dr. Brown's office.

DR. BROWN

Jeff, I have the results of all your tests, and I cannot find any observable reasons for your condition.

JEFF

(in a disappointed tone)

Doctor, look at them.

(holding out his hands)

I cannot bend my hands or fingers. What can be the cause?

DR. BROWN

In my opinion, you have glove
anesthesia.

JEFF

What is that?

DR. BROWN

Glove anesthesia is a conversion
hysterical disorder. Such disorders
may occur when an individual is
emotionally upset or, as we doctors
say to our patients, completely
stressed out. This overwhelming
stress causes glove anesthesia, which
is a paralysis of the hands.

JEFF

Doctor, why did this paralysis affect
my hands and fingers and not some
other part of my body?

DR. BROWN

Because whatever was bothering you
up to the time of your glove
anesthesia had something to do with
hand and finger movement.

JEFF

I think I understand. Maybe that is why I could not put the wedding ring on Victoria's finger.

DR. BROWN

I want to set up two therapeutics sessions a week for you, and keep that schedule until the problem is solved.

JEFF

OK, Doctor. I will make the appointments. Thank you.

Jeff leaves the office.

JEFF

(speaking to himself)

Hmmm, maybe I can work this out on my own.

Lights off.

<u>Scene 2</u>

Lights on. Jeff is sitting at the breakfast table with his mom and Aunt Esther.

MOTHER

Jeff, you look wonderful and well
rested.

AUNT ESTHER

Let me serve you some flavored
coffee. It is your favorite.

JEFF

Thanks.

*Jeff stands up and leaves the breakfast table. He
walks around the stage trying to move his hands
and fingers.*

JEFF

(speaking to himself)

I am beginning to feel comfortable
around Mom and Aunt Esther again. I
have noticed that some feeling has
returned to both hands and some
fingers. I will wait a little longer to
make an appointment with Dr.
Brown. Let's see how things go.
Maybe the problem will go away on
its own.

Lights. Later that day.

Jeff is in his bedroom at his mother's house.

JEFF

(speaking to himself)

This is great! I can move my hands and fingers like before. It looks like I have conquered this glove anesthesia. I am going to start painting again right away.

Jeff walks off the stage.

VOICE OF JEFF

Mom, I will be in the studio.

Lights off.

<u>Scene 3</u>

Lights on. Victoria knocks on the door of Mother Agnes's house.

MOTHER

(Opening the door)

What do you want? You have no business here!

VICTORIA

I must see Jeff. I need to talk with him.

MOTHER AGNES

(screaming)

He is not home, and don't come around here anymore. You will just upset the family. Now get off my property immediately! I order you!

Jeff hears the commotion and goes to the front door to see what is happening.

JEFF

Victoria!

VICTORIA

Jeff!

Jeff and Victoria hug. The mother slams the door on Jeff and Victoria.

VICTORIA

Jeff, let's walk to the park. I have wanted to talk with you, but I was so hurt about what happened at the church. I didn't think you wanted to see me.

JEFF

My lovely Victoria, I understand. I wanted to call you, but I have been so embarrassed and fearful about contacting you. Would you like to start seeing each other again?

VICTORIA

Yes, yes! I love you and miss you so much.

JEFF

Let's keep walking. I don't want this day to end. I have to be with you.

VICTORIA

I feel the same.

They continue walking and holding hands.

Lights off.

<u>Scene 4</u>

Lights on. Jeff enters his mother's house.

MOTHER

We saw you holding hands with Victoria. Don't tell me you reconciled with that little tramp.

AUNT ESTHER

Don't you dare disgrace your good family name. That Victoria is a poor excuse for a lady.

Jeff stands in the middle of the stage while his mom and Aunt Esther leave the stage yelling.

MOTHER

She is a hussy and a whore!

AUNT ESTHER

Nothing more than a streetwalking floozy!

JEFF

(yelling at them)

I am so fed up with you two!

Lights off.

Scene 5

Lights on. Jeff, his mother, and Aunt Esther are sitting at the dining room table.

AUNT ESTHER

Tell me, Jeff, how is Victoria? I mean the floozy Victoria.

MOTHER

Jeff, I did not hear you talking to the whore last night. Was something wrong with her phone?

AUNT ESTHER

Maybe she was busy setting up appointments with her customers.

The mother and Aunt Esther both laugh.

JEFF

Damn women! Stop it!

MOTHER

(In an innocent tone)

Does the truth hurt?

JEFF

I am leaving!

Jeff leaves the room and calls Victoria.

JEFF

We need to see each other. Please come by my house and pick me up. I will tell you later what is happening here.

(pause)

Thank you. I will see you in ten minutes.

Jeff sees Victoria and hugs her.

JEFF

It is so wonderful to be with you! I have good news. My hands and fingers are no longer paralyzed.

VICTORIA

That makes me so happy.

JEFF

My psychiatrist said that if I could get rid of my stress, then the problem would take care of itself. Victoria, you bring me peace and tranquility.

(Jeff kisses her hand).

You are good for my mental health. I love you. Let's go out for dinner on Friday and celebrate our reconciliation.

VICTORIA

Jeff, I wish I could, but my uncle died, and the whole family is leaving Friday afternoon to attend the funeral. We are planning to stay until Sunday to grieve and support the family.

JEFF

I understand. You should go.

Lights off.

<u>Scene 6</u>

Lights on. Breakfast at the dining room table.

MOTHER

Jeff, you are the most ungrateful person I have ever known. I have sent you to the best schools in the country, and this is how you repay me?

Jeff continues eating.

MOTHER

You are becoming one the best young painters in the country, and you want to lower yourself by marrying that shameless hussy.

AUNT ESTHER

She is not even pretty. People say all brides are pretty. Well, she is not one bit pretty. She looks ugly to me. Agnes, do you remember her wedding dress? It was so tight on her that it made her look cheap. I bet she bought it at a resale store.

MOTHER

She is cheap! C-h-e-a-p! Do you hear me, son? Your girlfriend is cheap.

The mother and Aunt Esther laugh as they leave the room.

Jeff is alone on the stage walking back and forth.

JEFF

(speaking to himself)

I could stage a crime scene and make it look like the motive of the intruders was a burglary. The intruders will kill my mom and aunt when they see them so they won't risk being recognized. This plan will work out just fine. The investigators will conclude that they had to choke them to death because they had no weapons. It will look like a burglary gone wrong. I will wait until late Saturday night to carry out my plan because they will both be asleep at that time.

Jeff moves his hands around with ease.

JEFF

I better get some rest. I have a lot going on this weekend.

Later that evening.

Jeff is pacing back and forth in his pajamas.

JEFF

(speaking to himself)

I cannot sleep. I am starting to feel guilty just thinking about doing such a terrible thing, but I have to do it.

Jeff walks toward his mother's bedroom.

JEFF

(speaking to himself)

It is the only solution. It is the only way I can have peace in my life. First, I will choke my mother to death. Then I will go to my aunt's bedroom and do the same to her.

Jeff tries to turn the doorknob, but he can't. His hands and fingers are paralyzed again. He quickly returns to his bedroom.

JEFF

(speaking to himself)

I have to do it! I have to! But how can I without the use of my hands?

Later that day.

Jeff is alone in his bedroom.

JEFF

(speaking to himself)

I still cannot move my hands or fingers. Maybe this is some sort of message. I better call Dr. Brown.

Jeff calls the doctor with his phone's voice activation.

JEFF

Dr. Brown, this is Jeff. I need to see you right away.

DR. BROWN

Jeff, why have you waited so long to make an appointment with me? I am rather busy right now.

JEFF

Doctor, this is a matter of life and death. I had a strong urge to choke my mother and aunt to death. Before I could go through with it, my glove anesthesia came back. My hands and

fingers are paralyzed. If the paralysis
goes away completely, I am afraid
that I will not be able to control my
urge to kill them.

DR. BROWN

It is not safe for you to drive, so I
want you to call a cab and come to
my office immediately.

JEFF

Thank you, Doctor.

DR. BROWN

Don't change your mind. What you
are experiencing is very serious.
Don't delay; I will be here waiting for
you.

Lights off.

<u>Scene 7</u>

Lights on. Jeff is at the doctor's office.

DR. BROWN

Jeff, I am glad you opened up to me
in greater detail about the
overwhelming stress and anger you

feel toward your mother and aunt. I
am very concerned about the rage
you feel toward them. This is getting
out of control.

JEFF

(standing up, very nervous)

Yes, Doctor. I know it is.

DR. BROWN

You would have likely followed
through with your impulse to kill
them. We can't be sure that your
mind will always be successful in
keeping the paralysis from returning
and consequently making it
impossible to choke them. I am going
to prescribe some medication that
will reduce your rage and get it under
control. Fill this prescription right
away, and take the pills as prescribed.
I can't force you to take them, but if
you don't take them, there is nothing
further I can do for you.

JEFF

Doctor, what we speak about is confidential. Am I correct?

DR. BROWN

Yes, you are correct. We psychiatrists are bound by our code of ethics not to betray our patients' confidence.

JEFF

(with a look of relief on his face)

Good. Thank you, Doctor.

DR. BROWN

One more thing, Jeff. You must move out of your mother's house so you can completely avoid your mother and aunt.

JEFF

No problem, Doctor. I've already found an apartment. I am moving out tomorrow.

Later that day.

Jeff and Victoria are sitting on a park bench.

JEFF

Let's get married but not have an
elaborate wedding.

VICTORIA

That is fine with me. We can keep it
very simple.

JEFF

Yes, let's do it.

Lights off.

ACT III

<u>Scene 1</u>

Lights on. The mother enters her living room.

MOTHER

(looking upset)

I was at the beauty shop, and I overheard that Jeff and that woman are getting married.

AUNT ESTHER

My God! We have to do something quickly. Think, sister, think!

MOTHER

Now I know why that ungrateful son of mine has not come to visit us.

AUNT ESTHER

Not even a phone call, and he promised he would keep in touch.

MOTHER

He is getting married, and he is trying to avoid us so he won't have to say anything about the wedding.

AUNT ESTHER

He does nothing for us and
everything for that shameless hussy.

MOTHER

Yes, I bet she has soured him on us.
All we ever wanted to do is protect
him.

AUNT ESTHER

I was thinking last night that Jeff is
old enough to stand up like a man—

MOTHER

(interrupting)

I know. He does not even have the
strength to—

AUNT ESTHER

(interrupting)

He was strong and listened to us until
he met that—

MOTHER

(interrupting)

Yes—that poor excuse of a woman.

AUNT ESTHER

Sister, you are the thinker. The wedding is in a few days. You have to come up with something.

MOTHER

The first thing I am going to do is call that vixen and give her a piece of my mind.

Lights off.

Scene 2

Lights on. Victoria is knocking on Jeff's apartment door.

JEFF

(opens the door)

Hello, Victoria. What's going on? Why are you crying? Come in and tell me what happened.

VICTORIA

Your mother called me.

JEFF

What did she say?

VICTORIA

(crying harder)

She said that if I married you...

JEFF

Don't cry, baby.

VICTORIA

Oh, Jeff! She sounded so hateful and vindictive. She knows all about the wedding.

JEFF

(hugging Victoria)

I don't care if she knows. Please, honey, tell me what she said.

VICTORIA

She said that if marry you, my family will regret it. Jeff, I am truly scared.

JEFF

If she calls you again, don't answer
the phone. I will take care of this.
How dare her! Stop crying, baby.

VICTORIA

I am trying, Jeff. I am just so upset.
We really need to take care of each
other.

JEFF

Don't worry about it. I will talk to you
later. I love you.

VICTORIA

I love you too. Bye.

Victoria walks off the stage.

Lights off.

<u>Scene 3</u>

*Lights on. Mother Agnes and Aunt Esther are
knocking on Jeff's apartment door. Jeff opens the
door but tries to close it when he sees them. They
push their way inside the apartment.*

MOTHER

(looking around)

Jeff, my house is better than this apartment. You don't even have a studio to do your painting, and the lighting is terrible in here.

AUNT ESTHER

Listen to us, Jeff. We have our reasons for coming here.

MOTHER

We are here to put some sense into your head. Cancel the wedding!

JEFF

(screaming)

Mom and Aunt Esther, listen to me. I love Victoria. You are not going to stop me from marrying her. Under no circumstance will I cancel the wedding. I want you two to leave my apartment immediately.

MOTHER

Then I will stop you right now!

Mother Agnes takes a gun out of her purse and shoots Jeff.

                    AUNT ESTHER

                    (screaming)

Sister, you killed our boy!

                    MOTHER

Shut up! It is his fault for not listening to us.

                    AUNT ESTHER

(kneeling over Jeff's body)

Jeff, my baby, we only wanted the best for you. We always loved you.

                    MOTHER

Is he dead?

                    AUNT ESTHER

                    (standing up)

Yes, he stopped breathing. You killed him.

(crying and screaming)

You just killed your only child.

MOTHER

It's Victoria's fault, not mine. I never would have shot him if it were not for her trying to ruin his life. I saved him from a life of hell!

AUNT ESTHER

(screaming)

Give me the gun! You have gone too far!

MOTHER

No!

Aunt Esther tries to grab the gun from her sister. The mother shoots her during the struggle for the gun.

The stage is almost completely dark. The mother sits on the floor between the two dead bodies.

MOTHER

(speaking to herself in a sad tone)

Now I am all alone.

The stage is completely dark. A gunshot is heard.

VOICE OF A MAN ON THE TELEVISION

In today's top story, a promising
young painter and two older women
were found dead in an apartment this
morning. The police are investigating.

Lights slowly dim.

Also by this author:

Searching for Cibola

Not from Here, Not from There

Denial, Confrontation, Obsession and Return

The Golden Years?

Revenge or Forgiveness?

In Time, Malinche, In Time

Medicine Woman

Shadow Enemies

Personality Psychology 235